RISING ABOVE
THE BEAUTY OF LIFE

Copyright 2011 - 2nd edition
All rights reserved. No part
of this work may be reproduced without
written permission from the author.

www.beautifulwarrior.com

DOLORES M. MILLER
POET & AUTHOR

ACKNOWLEDGEMENT TO MY FAMILY
The Power of Love

When I think of my family, I think of Love. I love the three of you very much!

I realize now how hard it must have been on the three of you when I was facing those horrid memories. Working through all that anger is one of the hardest things I ever faced. I also want to thank the three of you for supporting me and loving me enough with your compassion and understanding.

I know you all must have had your own anger. It is OK. I am not afraid to hear whatever you need to express to me. I am here with an open heart and open mind. My love for the three of you, my love of life and my faith in God and myself got me through it all.

I learned one very important lesson. The power of Love is stronger than any hate or anger. That is why I was determined to keep healing, working, and overcoming. I am thankful that God gave me a strong spirit. The worst is all behind. Life is beautiful! I have become the strong, creative, woman I was always meant to be!

Yes, in our life there will be times of pain and times of sorrow, but the love we have for each other and the beauty of life and all its magnificence will shine through. Finally, I hope and pray through my writing that I will help make this world a better place for you, my husband, son, daughter, all my nieces and nephews, and all future generations.

ACKNOWLEDGEMENTS

Mom & Dad
Thank you for adopting me out of a horrific situation and showing us (all of your children) Christmas Joy and Love. Even though you are in Heaven mom, I know you hear me. I want to thank you and daddy from the bottom of my heart.

Dr. Bonnie Frank Carter
I am so thankful you supported me and believed in me during the healing process! I have an appreciation for your firmness, truthfulness and kindness during a very difficult time. You went above and beyond.

Melanie McLaughlin, my teacher and friend, my sister Gail, as well as, my sisters-in-law: Helen, Dee, Annie, Laura and all of my girlfriends – who stuck by me through good times and bad times. I cherish each and every one of you!

Book Review

Abuse victim. Just seeing these words can be enough to make just about anyone freeze, flee or prepare to fight. However we hear the facts as a fellow victim, a friend, a teacher, an attorney or as the therapist, all witnesses struggle with the same questions. Does anyone ever "get over" the violation of abuse, especially when the ones who do the hurting are the same people who were supposed to be protecting us? Can anyone really have a good adulthood when childhood included early experiences too horrible to put into words? Dolores M. Miller offers us the unequivocal answer that "Yes," it surely is possible to enjoy the Good that Life offers, no matter what has gone before.

With writings created during her personal journey from victimized child to someone surviving and on to thriving adult, Dolores gives us direct evidence of a true life "happy ending." In letters to dear friends and family, poetic musings on nature, and loving prayers to the powers of the Universe, she illustrates many of the steps she took to reclaim the shining path of light and love that is her true birthright.

And how does someone get from the victim experience onward to thriving adulthood? By crying, sobbing, and screaming out loud, by raging and by writing, by expressing the horror, the sadness, the longing and the anger until all the parts are heard, loud and clear and usually then to repeat these very same steps, often more than once, because some things still have not been heard enough. Eventually, it becomes possible to "smell the roses" once again.

It was my privilege to support Dolores through some of these difficult avenues on her recovery journey. I thereby have the honor to bear witness to the strong and secure place she inhabits now, a psychological and spiritual space where she savors all the joys - great and small - that life offers, where she encourages herself and others when the journey of life includes bumps and bruises as are inevitable to the human condition, and where she generously shares Lessons she has gleaned along the way.

And so, just as Dee oftentimes would get a morning coffee to warm her as she worked towards her truest and best Life, I invite you to get yourself a cup of something warming to sip as you reach into the lovely treasure before you. As surely as the day follows night and "...on the shores of darkness there is light" (John Keats, To Homer), this volume offers real life evidence of one childhood victim who has achieved thriving adulthood. And where there is one, there can be many. We all can benefit by carrying within us this encouragement and support from Dolores M. Miller as we move through a Life that may often times require us to bear witness to the strength and possibility of the human spirit.

In peace, and with all that is good,
Bonnie Frank Carter, PhD

Wayne, PA

DEDICATION

To my husband: Larry
Thank you for never giving up on me –
For always believing in me,
standing by me and showing me
the true meaning of love.

I Locked Away My Heart
Twenty First Love Letter

Time... it goes by so quickly.

I watch the sadness of my father yearning for my mother,
Love prevails and finds comfort for the soul, into eternity
They will meet again one day.

Crying now at the thought of ever losing you,
my charming knight in armor.
Only Time will know who goes first.
Here or hereafter, I locked away my heart.
It will always be saved for you.

Your kindness destroyed the harshness in this life.
Sunlight will remain in the fibers of my being.
Its light has helped me to see the beautiful, talented, creative
person who was always there.

So... while we are here,
let's live each day as if it were our last,
enjoying all of its splendor and beauty.
Loving, hoping and reaching out to suffering souls.
Laughing, dancing and having fun.

It is so good to be alive!

FORWARD

Dear Mom,
We want to express how proud we are of your work and your dedication to complete this book!

As your family, we have witnessed your transformation as transcribed on these pages. It has not always been smooth, but through your faith and will you have always managed to follow the healthier road using your inner warrior strength to push through even the most challenging times.

What is really amazing is your ability not only to heal yourself, but also to help heal others along the way. This is truly a gift from God. Your energy and passion for life inspire those around you. Your positive attitude has encouraged people who have lost hope. Your unique character has helped others embrace their own individualism.

This book is truly a testament to your compassion and commitment to help others. It is a gift that will continue to give for as long as this universe exists.

As a wife and mother, you have never let us down!

Thank You, from the bottom of our hearts, for never giving up. Your determination ripples through in our happiness! Thank you for teaching us that even in the darkest times, hope remains.

We Love You!
Larry, Larry & Michele

Dolores lives with her Knight in Shining armor, Larry, and together they have two grown children, Larry (Jones) and Michele – who she loves with all of her heart.

APPROACH TO WORK:
I know in my heart that, no matter what a person faces in life, with God's healing love a person can overcome. I write with the knowledge that the Strength of the "Warrior Spirit" inside of us is stronger than any adversity.

PURPOSE:
To reach out, to all people so I can inspire and provide health, healing and spirituality... My healing words can touch deep inside, to the fibers of the soul. I want others to know if they keep believing, even when it is difficult they will rise above.

DIRECTION:
I will continue to write of God's healing love, hope, courage, and the beauty of nature: reaching out with my words to suffering souls, so they may find the power to heal... to become all they were meant to be.

TABLE OF CONTENTS

1. HEALING
2. WHAT LOVE CAN DO
3. THE BEAUTY OF LIFE
4. ABOUT THE AUTHOR
5. PUBLICATIONS & AWARDS
6. PRAISE AND ACCOLADES

HEALING

THE BEAUTIFUL WARRIOR	1
TRIBUTE TO THE BEAUTIFUL WARRIOR	2
LITTLE PRECIOUS ANGEL, LITTLE PRECIOUS GIRL	3
THE WONDERS OF GOD	4
LORD, I BELIEVE IN YOU	5
GOD IN HEAVEN	6
I LEFT THAT SHORE	7
STAYING THERE	8
EVEN THEM - THE PRISON MEN	9
DANCE OF ANGER	10
TEARS OF SADNESS TEARS OF JOY	11
THE MONSTER	12
LET ME OUT	13
SPEAK SOFTLY	14
A NEW EPITHET	15
ROLLER COASTER	16
COURAGE	17
DID YOU SEE HER?	18
TAKE OFF THE BLINDERS	19
HEY PEOPLE	20
THE ONE	21

I WILL ALWAYS GET TO MY DESTINATION	22
THAT DAD	24
THE GAZEBO BY THE SEA	26
HAPPY BIRTHDAY SWEET 16	27
KNIGHT IN SHINING ARMOR	28
HE LISTENS	29
MY MESSAGE TO THE HUMAN RACE	30
I LOVE YOU LITTLE GIRL	31
HE KEEPS SHOWING YOU THE WAY	32
SHORT AND SWEET	33
MY CHRISTMAS PRAYER	34
WHEN I THINK OF HER	35
HAPPY EASTER, HAPPY SPRING	36
HAPPY THANKSGIVING	37
FRANCES	38
I FELT GOD'S LOVE	39
YOU HAVE ONE LIFE HERE	40
OUR COUSIN PAT	41
HELP ONE MORE CHILD TODAY	42
I BELIEVE IN YOUR COMPASSION	44
BEAUTY	45
A TOUCH OF HEAVEN	46
THE BEACH IS WHERE I GO TO PRAY	47
LIKE THE DOLPHINS	48

DANCING	49
THE FRANKLIN GALAXY BALL	50
THE GRAND CANYON	51
THE ROCKY MOUNTAINS	52
GRACE MY VANCOUVER FRIEND	53
THE HAWAIIAN DANCERS	54
TO YOU, VIRGINIA WOOLF	55
REFLECTION	56
BEAUTIFUL BLUE ARIZONA SKIES	57
PHOENIX, ARIZONA	57
NEW HOPE	58
RISING ABOVE THE BEAUTY OF LIFE	59
ALASKA	59
ALASKA'S MS RYNDAM	60
HOLLAND AMERICA LINE	60
PUBLICATIONS & AWARDS	66

****

HEALING

THE BEAUTIFUL WARRIOR

You, You precious child,
have dealt with so much of the pain.
The horror was horrible then.
Sweet child it was never you!

The war has been over for a long time.
I am showing you the beauty of your life now:
You can trust and believe again.

You are stronger, wiser, a true survivor,
"Treasures out of the darkness,"
is what The Bible says.
You are like a beautiful warrior...
Brave and Free.

TRIBUTE TO THE BEAUTIFUL WARRIOR

I know you must have felt
such deep despair,
when you saw that no one
was coming there.

No one came to release you
from such horrible pain,
you were beaten and raped,
had no way to escape.

Oh Beautiful Warrior,
most precious child*,
somehow, you survived
such terror---
Your choice was life,
even in such unbelievable
fright.

I want to show the world
her strength and beauty,
how she rose above . . .
how inside her (even then)
was courage, hope and love.

I want to show her
that the war has been over
for a long, long time . . .
she is a Beautiful Warrior
Brave and Free.

*A message from me as an adult to myself as a child.

LITTLE PRECIOUS ANGEL, LITTLE PRECIOUS GIRL

Little girls are supposed to play
and wear pretty dresses,
and know they are loved.

Little girls are not supposed
to be beaten and raped.

Little precious angel, I want you know
you were in a war of hell*.

I am so sorry that he was nuts,
and angry and cruel.

I want you to know that now I can
help you heal. That you are loved
and you were always loveable*.

I want you to know that you were so
brave and that I can teach you to
trust and to be all you can be.

Love, Joy, Hope and Healing!
"I wish for you always!"

*A message from me as an adult to myself as a child.

THE WONDERS OF GOD
They are inside of you
Dedicated to the Beautiful Survivors

Inside of you is a child
who was meant to fly,
to learn all the horribleness
was a bunch of big lies,
you had the strength to
live and survive.

Inside of you,
Jesus can take away the pain,
of hurt, anger, fear and shame.
His cleansing love can purify,
He wants you whole
and fully alive.

The journey is long,
Oh, God I know how tough;
sometimes I wonder:
How long do I have to go through this much?
But inside of you is mighty strong stuff.

The wonders of God, they are inside of you,
His strength, love and kindness,
will help to make you anew.

The wonders of God,
have helped me to see,
to never give up,
to be all He wants you to be.
It's a message of love,
to help set you free.

You are all like roses
constantly unfolding.

LORD, I BELIEVE IN YOU

Lord, I will never stop believing in you,
and the strength you gave me inside.

It was a horrible nightmare.
Lord, Why?
I'm tired of asking.
How did I survive such terror?

I worked through and faced, so many hard things.
I'm tired Lord,
but I will never
give up.

I have a wonderful life here.
I finally realize:
The war has been over for a long time.
No one will ever hurt me like that again.
No one has for a long, long time.

There are so many wonderful people here.
Wonderful people who made up for such ugliness.
I'm not afraid anymore.
It's OK to cry from relief sometimes.

Your love and grace has gotten me this far.
I am moving on to new horizons.
You are molding me into the creative, loving,
adventurous woman I was intended to be.
Lord, I believe in You!

GOD IN HEAVEN

"God in Heaven", help them all,
All the children, who stood tall.
In the midst of adults who couldn't deal,
with their hurt and pain,
who had an innocent child living there,
who had to deal with their despair.

Please give them the Courage,
to realize there is a God above,
who can heal with his wondrous love,
who wants to help and make them whole.
To let them know that their strength,
has made them bold.

I'm writing to let those Precious Angels know,
there are people here,
that they can trust who really care.
To let their hearts really believe,
that they can be free,
from chaos and
insanity.

I LEFT THAT SHORE

I left that shore,
of long ago winds,
I went to the shore
of Hope.
I adjusted the sails,
on my boat,
The winds were strong,
I decided to coast.

Looking in a different direction,
I could see:
The sunset, the birds,
glittering of beauty on the trees.
The joy of knowing,
It Is Time To Be Free.

Once I saw,
the other shore,
It became easier to not drift,
back to before.
Sailing where I wanted . . .
More and More.

I adjusted that sail
so many times,
It helped me see
that new shore was finally mine.
Decided to go to the shore,
That Would Be My Home
For Evermore!

STAYING THERE
Looking

Looking...
at the glittering raindrops,
on the trees.
Reminds me once again
I'm finally free.
Worked through so much,
"GOD it was so TOUGH!"

Stronger, it put my spirit, to the test.
Realize, I am not like the rest.

No, I decided . . .
Instead of feeling sorry for myself,
Put those old feelings, on the shelf.
Throw them away!

Ain't going to ask anymore,
Why I had to break through that door.
"I Did, I'm Alive",
Survived, Thriving, Rising.
Reached up to the sky,
I am whole, and fully alive!

Not Just Looking . . .
To another shore,
Staying There!
Where there is Love, Joy, and Care.

Looking at myself,
in a different light.
I see wings that are colorful
and bright!

Staying There!

EVEN THEM - THE PRISON MEN

Even them, the prison men,
Don't tolerate the monster man.

If they find out one
is within the prison walls,
They make sure he gets his due.

They let him know with no mistake,
That they really hate
The one who rapes. (especially children)

No matter what they choose to do ---
The bastard deserves it
Through and through!

If they choose to beat him unmercifully,
rape him, cut him . . . or kill him.

Then he can never hurt another child... again.

DANCE OF ANGER
Dance With Me

Sometimes the Anger is like a flame . . .
It is the flame of injustice, and the rain
Of Past Horrid Pain!

I Will Not Let It Get Me Down ---

I will take the flame, turn it around
use it, as a standing ground.

My pen is my sword.
It is a source of Light, It will take the flame,
and make it the Dance of Right.

The Dance of Anger, Let it tell of Truth and Justice ---

I'm Speaking Out for every person, (child or adult)
It is their right!
To live a life of Peace and Joy!

Dance With Me
Help Stop the war, of Abuse and Violence!
Please Listen! Do Your Part!

Dance With Me!!

TEARS OF SADNESS TEARS OF JOY

There were tears of sadness,
that I have cried so many times,
for the little girl, (me then)
the pain and horror she went through.

There were tears of sadness,
that I have cried so many times,
for me now, all the healing,
and hard work I went through.

But, now there are tears of Joy,
of relief and renewal.
Knowing the worst is over,
seeing myself in a NEW light.

"It is time to stop the rain,
turn the tide."
"Beautiful Warrior,"
you are becoming the woman,
you were always meant to be.

THE MONSTER

What kind of human being . . .
-- No -- Monster --
could do the things he did?
His horrible laugh, he was from the pits of hell!
I am still here, I am still Alive.
I believe in God and Myself!
That monster is dead!!!!
I want to tell the survivors of that horrible monster.
You are stronger, you are wiser, don't let him win!

LET ME OUT

Let me out; let me out of the f___ing nut house.
I can see her banging the window*---
Oh please don't leave; I don't want to deal with
the nutty insanity!
Oh Beautiful Warrior, Beautiful Child,
No wonder you blocked it so long,
It was so horrible and wild.

You have dealt with anger and
so much pain, now you have learned
It wasn't your blame. You have been free
from the nut house for a long, long time.
I will love you and defend you,
and show you how you have survived.

Because you are strong, because
you are bright, you had the determination
inside you to live and survive. But now,
one by one, You have let the guards down.
For a long, long time,
The nut has been dead . . .

Yes, you are free, free to be all you
were supposed to be.
You also help me to see
how proud I am to be me.

*A message from me as an adult to myself as a child.

SPEAK SOFTLY

Speak softly
when you speak
of the warrior,
child of light.

The pieces
of her heart
were broken.

God took the pieces,
and molded them into,
his most
Magnificent Work of Art.

A most loving
and courageous Heart,
That dreams of a world
with more Love, Hope, and Compassion.

This Heart will do its part,
to help make A Better World!

A NEW EPITHET

What a Revolution!
The seeds that have been dormant
Are springing forth and growing.

The healing journey has shown
the strength, creativity, and beauty.
The cultivating of my own Garden
has burst forth into new light.

No more will I let, paint by number lives,
that lack feeling and emotion,
to clip at my most colorful garden.

No more needing approval from others.
I have the right, to be creative, beautiful and different.
To say, Feel it and Live it.

Out of the mud, there has burst forth Glory!

ROLLER COASTER
Ride In The Sky

I took a roller coaster ride in the sky.

Went through a rain storm.

Just like different times in my life.

Each situation showed a trust an assurance.

That the landing was always graceful always fine,

it was His Peace, His Love.

COURAGE

Beautiful Warrior, don't lose sight
of how far you came.
Just like in the movie "Alive",
they continued on.
Even when the
winds grew strong.

Beautiful Wings, Courageous Wings

No matter what else,
You are going to face.
Your courage inside,
set the pace.
To knowing you have left,
that shore of long ago.
To see the sun rise and sun set,
that alone breaks through any pain.

You are here and Alive,
there is nothing so wonderful,
as Life.
Love and Admiration are yours,
courageous one.

DID YOU SEE HER?
Take the Time to Find Her

Did you see her?
That Beautiful Warrior of Light.
who has eyes that blaze like Amethysts . . .
The light from them has burned through the darkness.
She can see a new Horizon.

In her soul was embroidered Colors,
that adversity could not break.
They are colors of Courage, Hope and Love.
God in His amazing Grace,
Sent them from above.

Riding on her golden horse into
New Life,
Wonderful Meaning,
and Blessed Liberation.
Yes, I saw her because she
is the warrior in me,
she is also in You!
Take the time
to Find her!

TAKE OFF THE BLINDERS

When will they take off the blinders of prejudice?
"I hate niggers is what they say" ---
Do they ever really see what such ignorance breeds?
Corruption, condemnation and sorrow,
that will impede a bright tomorrow.

PLEASE THINK OF THE CHILDREN!

When will they take off the blinders of not knowing?
"Well I don't understand is what they say" ---
so why is he acting that way?
He's crazy, he's lazy but I don't look at me,
what I will find will be hard to see ---
denial, regret and dishonesty.

PLEASE THINK OF THE CHILDREN!

When will they take off the blinders of no I can't change?
My father abused me so I'll do the same ---
It is time to look inside, it is time to break the chain,
of hurt, anger, confusion and blame.

PLEASE THINK OF THE CHILDREN!

HEY PEOPLE
Don't Be Afraid To Look Inside

Hey People anywhere,
I want you to know, that I really care,
you see...
Already faced such pain, like a knife through my being...
Developed a different way of seeing.

When I see a red rose or bright autumn leaves,
a baby smiling or feel a warm, summer breeze...
My talents or creativity, the love of my children and family.
Then I knew it was worth all my fight, to work for a life that I deserve.

So, Hey People anywhere,
who are facing any pain or sorrow,
You also deserve a better tomorrow.
Yeah, you might feel, like you will go crazy,
Might feel like you want to die . . .
but God's Holy Grace, will help you survive.

Then like a piece of wood, that was carved and formed,
You will become like a work of art, that was remade and reborn.

So for people who get caught up with glitter and fame,
Worry about getting Old, Wrinkles and are Vain.
Get A Life!

Don't be afraid to look inside, and see the Strong, Beautiful Human Being, that was always there.

THE ONE

He is the One who can bring new life,
cleanse your heart and rescue you from strife.

He is a representation of my ability,
to transform, liberate and set my soul free.

Talking about Jesus my true best friend,
you have helped me to heal
and to find who I am.

Friend, I want you to share
my joy, my vigor and genuine care---

He's the One, it's up to you!

Today, keep Love in your life and a Smile on your face!

I Will Always Get to My Destination

There is a reverence,
there is a Joy,
Colorado
Trees with a white blanket of snow,
bring the beauty and courage of
the Beautiful Warrior to the surface.

Trying new things -
Snowshoeing.

It is yet another way to be so close to nature.
To be alive, to know with complete certainty
I will always be OK.
The weathering of every snow storm,
showed my imperishable courage.

Like a frozen pond,
that no matter what might come along,
reflects joy, peace and my heart filled with compassion
to do what I can to make a
change for a better world.

A knowing that life
even with its twists and turns
like my snowshoes,
I will always get to my destination.
Called who I am
and called home.

The believing of a future
that can only be like
the ice on the trees,
glittering and bright.

WHAT LOVE CAN DO

THAT DAD

Daddy, what you and mom did was
of more value than anything in the whole world.

When you and mom adopted me
out of that horrible place,
and raised me and showed me love -
that dad was priceless.

When each year at Christmas,
you and Mom made Christmas joy
for me and my brothers and sister, -
that dad was priceless.

I know we have our differences,
because you see dad,
I am very strong willed like you;
I also have a great big heart like you!

So you see dad,
you already gave all the riches in the world
to all your children... -
that dad money can't buy.

ANGEL WINGS

Gentle breeze,
softness on my face,
Gently shaking the trees,
calmness, peace, and celebration!

As I sit, on my front step,
looking up to the star studded sky,
I think again,
it is so good
To be alive!

Gentle breeze,
coming through my screen filled window,
Can you be, the touch of an Angel's wing?

Then I pray that any child,
who is hurting out there,
that some way, they will feel my love,
and the softness of the Gentle breeze . . .
Angel wings.

THE GAZEBO BY THE SEA
This poem is dedicated to my loving son Larry

The Gazebo by the sea
Reminds me of what he did for me ---
He held me there when I was in pain,
helped heal my heart, and stopped the rain.

He showed me love beyond compare.
It gave me courage and helped make me aware,
that even on the darkest days . . .
The sun will shine tomorrow.

Now I sit here and all I see,
Is beauty and tranquility.
Because of that day by the sea,
His love has helped to set me free.

HAPPY BIRTHDAY SWEET 16
3rd Angel Letter

Happy Birthday, Sweet 16.
With all your beauty,
style and gleam.

Daddy and I
are so proud to be,
the parents of such,
joy and creativity.

Sometimes it is so
hard to believe,
that such an Angel,
came down from Heaven,
to her father and me.

Now it's so
hard to believe,
that our little girl is "Sweet 16!"
A young Woman.
We LOVE you!

"Happy Birthday Sweet 16!"
Mom, Dad & Larry

KNIGHT IN SHINING ARMOR
8th Love Letter

You are my Knight in Shining Armor,
you came to rescue me.
Your Love, Strength and Kindness,
has helped set me free.

You are my Knight in Shining Armor,
I can see your radiant light,
you have helped me turn all the wrongs,
into meaningful, beautiful rights.

Through you, my Knight in Shining Armor,
I have witnessed God's never ending love.
You helped me let go of hell, and shown me heaven above.

Our Love . . .
knows no bounds.
Our Love . . .
Depth and perception.

HE LISTENS
This poem is also extended to the other gracious people in my life, whose love and support will long be remembered.

He listens to horror and when I tell of the pain
sometimes I am frightened he lets me explain.

I tell him what I had to do then, to survive.
I tell him what I had to do then, to stay alive.

But does he realize when he listens ---
that he is helping to set me free,
that he is showing
compassion and humanity.

Oh Larry my husband
my true gentle friend.
You have taken this heart
and helped it to mend.

He listens . . . I know it's not easy,
thanks for showing me love,
true love.
I will be eternally grateful.

MY MESSAGE TO THE HUMAN RACE

It's Ok, I'm not afraid. I am going to tell what terror I faced. Even after all the healing and everything I faced and overcame, there are times I cry for the letter girl (me then)
She was so beautiful! One of the memories I had was the hurt and terror in her eyes. It did take WARRIOR strength to survive such an ordeal.
I have written about this before. I am not afraid to write about it again. Now I know all the terror was THEN. There is only beauty and exhilaration of my wonderful life NOW. I had many years of wonderful childhood. I was adopted out of that hell. There are so many children who lived with that terror all their life.
My message to the Human Race: If each person helps even one child who lived in abuse, it would make a BIG difference in this Beautiful, crazy, world.
Now when I think of the little girl, all I see is a Beautiful Warrior who had the courage and strength to RISE ABOVE, and heal. I have become the adventurous, creative woman I was always meant to be.
Thank you Lord for always being there, even when I felt you weren't.

Dedicated to my Courageous Mother, Peggy, who also faced a very hard ordeal. She is a survivor of Breast Cancer.

Note – This was written in 1996, my mom went with the Lord, June 25, 2005.

I LOVE YOU LITTLE GIRL

I love you little girl, you were so beautiful and brave.
I know it hurt little girl, the things that were done to you.

I am going to help you heal little girl,
Now that I know the terrible truth.

But know this ---
you were always beautiful, loving, creative and smart.
Living around them shattered your little heart.

My love, the love of my family and Jesus too ---
are going to help repair your precious heart, and make it new.

I am going to defend you, And mend you.
Stand up for your rights.

I am going to love you, and guide you . . .
With the help of my precious savior,
you will see the light.

His light breaks through any darkness.
His love repairs every pain.
He turns the rain into sunshine.
His love heals and saves.

I love you little girl,
he loves you little girl,
Your family does too.
I will tell you everyday
until you believe it is true.
Love, Joy and happiness,
Were always there for You!

HE KEEPS SHOWING YOU THE WAY
Dedicated to the Beautiful Warrior, the child of then, who was me. Also, His Love is Available for Anyone Who Wants It.

He will keep showing you the way, Beautiful Warrior
He will keep shining his Holy light.
You have come very far.
Beautiful Warrior, the Lord loves you with all His Might.

You will never get all the answers of Why,
you had to face that Plight,
but, when you Trust in The Lord,
with all your heart, he will make everything right.

Beautiful Warrior, the child of then,
I want you to know you couldn't have found, a better friend.
His name is Jesus.

SHORT AND SWEET

Do you know
I Love You So?
Does it Show?

Know this:

A LOVE like ours
Will Never Quit!

Short and Sweet
but so Complete.

I Love You So!

MY CHRISTMAS PRAYER
Please Pray For Them

At this Christmas Season,
with all its cheer,
hustle bustle.
Glory and Reason.
Please pray for them.

There are children
who will not,
have Christmas cheer.
Who instead of living
with Love and Joy,
live with Hate and Fear.
Please pray for them.

Oh, God, this is my prayer,
I pray that one day,
they will see,
that they can be
happy and free.
That there is Joy, not just Misery.
Please pray for them.

Merry Christmas,
Happy New Year.

Sending out this message so Clear ---
Oh, God from heaven above,
send down Hope to them,
Your Peace and Love!
Please pray for them.

WHEN I THINK OF HER
My Sister

Sisterhood is a special bond,
of friendship, open communication, and joy.
It is something, that cannot be measured.
It is one of life's most precious treasures.

When I think of my sister, I think of Love.
She stuck by me, through thick and thin.
Had the faith in me, that I would always win.

Thank you for the times . . .
you overlooked my "broken gate,
and saw the flowers in my garden."

Sister, this is a dedication to You . . .
throughout the rest of your precious life,
I wish you all the Happiness your heart can hold.

HAPPY EASTER, HAPPY SPRING
Rejoice

Think of the Love our Heavenly Father brings.
His loving Son, down to the earth,
to send us all joy and rebirth.
Rejoice! Rejoice! He Lives!

Like the flower that unfolds,
he can bring renewal to our souls.
Rejoice! Rejoice! He Lives!

Sending down HIS loving grace,
to put a smile upon our face.
Rejoice! Rejoice! He Lives!

Happy Easter, Happy Spring.
No matter what life might bring,
Your Heavenly Father sent your King!
Rejoice! Rejoice! He Lives!

HAPPY THANKSGIVING
10th Love Letter
Dedicated to Larry & Michele

There is no greater gift we can give our children
than the love we share for each other.

Thank you for your caring, not just for the children and me,
But when I would tell you of the Little girl (of then)
For always being a true gentle friend!

Happy Thanksgiving

Taking me wonderful places, I never dreamed I would see.
For encouraging, my individuality.
Helping me bloom, into the creative woman,
I was always meant to be.

Like the Pilgrims, I have found America in your Love.

Happy Thanksgiving

FRANCES

Frances was a positive influence in my life:
she helped me see with faith in myself,
"You can overcome strife."
She had a wonderful outlook –
"It's your attitude that makes you."
In good times or bad times . . .
The choice is yours.

She always took interest in who you were,
the strength she had was one of nerve.
"If you make your mind up there's nothing
you can't do." At the same time she understood
other people's pain, she tried to do it when
it was easier to refrain.

She loved art and music and having fun,
because she was my friend, I was the lucky one.
I'll miss her charm, her laughter and strength.
For the lady I had admiration and respect,
we can overcome and try to do our best.
Goodbye my friend . . .
Heaven's gates are open
for you.

I FELT GOD'S LOVE

She called me to tell me
her son was alright,
that he would be fine
from the accident last night.

Oh God I felt your love so near,
with her words that touched
my heart so dear.
You must of had your Guardian
Angels there.

In her I saw your gentle love;
don't worry, don't fret
He's OK,
she took my hurt and fears away.

Oh what is this, can it be,
a gentleness in humanity.
Oh thank you God for showing me,
that there is your love, Genuinely.

YOU HAVE ONE LIFE HERE
Live It Well

Dedicated to my friend Kathy Klinger
Another Beautiful Warrior

You have one life here, live it well.
Even though there are times, you might go through hell.

As a survivor, I want you to know the truth,
Rise Up, Rise Up.
Give it one last round,
trials can make you stronger,
or keep you down.

You can't change others,
you can only change you inside.
You can Rise Above and live,
a life with Pride.

You can face your fears,
work through your pain.
Realize your beauty,
and not take blame.

You have one life here, live it well.
You can focus on heaven, even through times of hell.

When someone acts,
a certain weird way,
Say "that's their problem,"
then enjoy your day.

You Have One Life Here, Live It Well.

OUR COUSIN PAT
Dedicated to Carol Comerford.
In loving memory of her sister Pat.
She was like a glorious Eagle, Beautiful and Strong.

Our Cousin Pat, most of her life,
was full of hurt, fear and strife.
Through all of it, she was full of
Fun, Style and Grace.

She lived her Life.

It didn't stop her
from going where,
she wanted to go.
From doing what,
she wanted to do.
From being Her.

She lived her Life.

There was so much love there.
With her sister and cousins,
shedding their tears.

The Lord took her to Heaven,
One crisp October Morn . . .
Now she will Continue,
Living Her Life Forever in Paradise.

HELP ONE MORE CHILD TODAY

I read her poem of a child with silent screams,
I am a survivor, I know what she means . . .

I cried, I thought, what bravery it took, to write such pain,
Then I stood up, and decided not to be afraid.

Instead of saying . . .

I wish no more children, had to face that plight.
I asked God to please hear my plea,
I got down on my knees.

I know abuse will never completely go away,
but dear God please, help one more child today.

All us survivors, must take a stand,
and help make it a better land.

I pray for any child, living in abuse today,
that one day, he will be free.

To heal, to love, to tell their whole story,
so their spirit and life will come into full glory.

The Beauty Of Life

I believe in Your Compassion

There is a sadness –
I am crying.
There are children
who go through abuse
every day,
and there are children
who die.

BUT, crying
will not bring change,
standing up
with my courage
and resources
to do my part -
all I can...
to make a change
for a better world.
that is the answer.

I am not afraid,
to ask you
to join me.
Have A Heart,
do Your Part,
big or small -
Help make a
brighter future
for children.
Let them know
that you care.

I Believe
in Your Compassion.

BEAUTY

Colors of the Autumn leaves,
frost laying on the trees,
feeling the Ocean breeze,
given the spirit of Peace & Tranquility.
That's what Beauty means to me.

A little Child, on Christmas Morn.
The day the Prince of Peace was born.
Glowing of the Christmas Trees,
eagles flying high and free.
That's what Beauty means to me.

When my little girl, said to me:
"Mommy you were always there,
Mommy you always cared."
That's what Beauty means to me.

Skiing down the mountain high.
Knowing I had the courage and strength to rise above.
Always having my Savior's and Husband's love.
That's what Beauty means to me.

A TOUCH OF HEAVEN
Dedicated to Ray and Anne

Vancouver was a touch of heaven . . .
Soaring over the mountains, helicopter in flight.
Wined and dined on their private yacht.
Oh what a delight.

They were a touch of heaven . . .
Both gentle, sweet and kind.
With life's toughness . . .
Yet so refined.

Nature was a touch of heaven . . .
Eagles above, trees around, water below.
Peace and tranquility, put on such a show.

The Vancouver Mountains were a touch of heaven . . .
Like me, they have strength and might,
the future holds promises, that can only be happy and bright.

Jesus, thank you for your healing and my wonderful gifts and opportunities.

THE BEACH IS WHERE I GO TO PRAY

The beach is where I go to pray ---
Commune with God in a special way,
the Place where ocean and earth meet,
this place where you can find inner peace.

The ocean sparkling from His bright blue sky ---
You can hear the wind you can feel the breeze,
I feel His love surrounding me.

It is His way of saying "I am here", "I do care"
you can always count on me.
I tell Him of my joys and pains,
Of what I lost and what I gained.

He shows me things that I can change,
I feel His love and joy and grace.
He lets me know with Him I'll see . . .
That I can be all He planned for me.

LIKE THE DOLPHINS

Such Wonder, those playful fun-loving Dolphins.
I Love Them!

Touching, splashing, feeding.
Becoming one with nature.
Tears of exultation.
The goodness and joy of life!

Trying new things,
keep breaking patterns.
How can we do it better?

We must . . .
Listen with our hearts.
Let's be like the Dolphins . . .
Seizing Every Day!
It is time to go,
to the Banquet of Life!

Blessed are the eyes that have dealt
with the reality
of hard and painful things,
but can also see
those special beautiful moments.
My writing has given me
so many of Those Moments . . .
Beauty, Wonder, Love.

Like The Dolphins!

DANCING

When I am dancing
I feel so free,
feel the music,
it's heavenly!

Let the music
fill your soul with melody,
it is beauty ---
rainbows of ecstasy.

Get into the groove:
dance, sing,
express your blessing
in Harmony.

Dancing is an art,
with style and grace.
Let yourself go,
in a wide open space.

When you dance,
you're free as a bird.
Spread your wings,
and get the nerve.

Dance and Sing . . .
Feel the joy that life can bring!

THE FRANKLIN GALAXY BALL

O beautiful,
wonderful enchantment
of the Franklin Galaxy Ball.
Lights, colorful lights,
shining, dancing,
just like the beautiful people
in gowns that sparkle
and suits that shine . . .

Dancing, laughing,
spreading their wings.
It's Electric,
one of the beautiful people say,
you did that dance so well . . .
then I smile knowing that the moments
I spent there were golden,
and wondrous as the lights,
shining, dancing,
and filling my heart and spirit
with the joy of life.

THE GRAND CANYON
Vastness, Beauty, Wonder

He has expressed
His artistry again!

Lord, Thanks,
it took my breath away!
You are the most magnificent artist,
in the universe.

For one brief moment . . .
I imagined I was an eagle,
soaring over and into the Grand Canyon.
Once again,
I felt Warrior Strength,
in my soul.

We, like the Indians,
should appreciate,
the Beauty of Nature,
and God's Natural Art Gallery!

THE ROCKY MOUNTAINS

There is splendor and beauty,
joy and delight,
they have a majesty about them,
courage and might.

My heart fills with awe,
as I watch the racers
with their speed ---
for a moment they dance in mid air,
with a sound that's so clear,
almost like a 747 in flight.

Oh Joy, Joy of being alive,
to see and hear beauty and flight,
if I lived for one hundred years,
I could not encounter such a time,
it will stay engraved in my heart
and always in my mind.

GRACE MY VANCOUVER FRIEND

Grace, my Vancouver friend,
you have shown me again,
what I already know.
What God's grace
and the Human Spirit can do,
to RISE above adversities.

Want you to know,
I had a wonderful Time,
in your most Amazing City . .

Mountains, harbors,
city of Artistic expression.
The city like you Grace,
like the flowers we both loved,
has left blossoming flowers in my heart!

Blossoming courage, creativity,
and an understanding-
that I only want to be around,
people who will help my garden grow.

THE HAWAIIAN DANCERS
New Year's Eve 1998

First we watched the
most graceful form
of loveliness
With
dark olive skin
swaying
her hips in
White.
She was Sensual and
Alluring.

Hula Dancer,
Beauty in Motion.

Then we watched the
fire dancer
With
his masculine delight,
dancing, throwing
Those
Knives of Fire.
It Was
A most heart pounding
Sight.

Fire Dancer,
Mana-Superhuman
feats of courage
in motion.

In the background
paradise
was putting on a
Show!

TO YOU, VIRGINIA WOOLF

Beautiful, Talented, Writer
wish I had known you.

Your wonderful book
"A Room of One's Own,"
has filled my heart,
with complete understanding.

You knew then in 1929
where women were supposed to be ---
non-conformists, even then.

You are right,
there will be a female Shakespeare.
"Fixed incomes and rooms of their own,"
unlocks the door.

Even though we're still not where we should be . . .
You, Virginia, would have been,
so much freer now,
to express your genius.

I wish you were here to experience it . . .

REFLECTION

Reflection
on
my
booklet.

Dancing colors,
purple,
green,
yellow,
red.

Reflection
from
my
glass stained windows.

It is so good to be Alive!

BEAUTIFUL BLUE ARIZONA SKIES
PHOENIX, ARIZONA
Dedicated to Linda and Jan Stache

I can hear them calling me
– the cry of Indians nearby.
Mountains in the distance.
Like a carved out frame on the earth.
I need to experience the Indian drums,
I feel the warrior strength rising up in my soul.
I see her again,
the mighty warrior of light
with amethyst eyes
riding on her horse into the sunset.

She is always there in my soul.
God has put her there to free my spirit,
free my mind,
and most of all
free my heart!

Arizona you always bring her to the surface
such joy and escalation!

NEW HOPE

*Dedicated to my Angel daughter, Michele,
Who also loves New Hope and is very creative.*

It's a place,
where,
All kinds of people
meet -
I need to go
and
Walk the streets
of New Hope.

There is so
much excitement there,
Motorcycle sounds
in the air.
Art and unique stores,
one can really explore.

Poetry slams
on Thursday nights.
The little town,
is out of sight.
It's a place
I can just be me.
Full of Life,
and creativity.

New Hope

RISING ABOVE THE BEAUTY OF LIFE
ALASKA

Can I say what I ponder
on this Journey today?
Alaska, Alaska,
Again
God shows His artistry -
the Crowning Glory of Alaska's Glacier Bay

Glaciers
crystals on blue.
The colors are not easily forgotten.
Harbor Seals,
bluish gray at the tip.

Ocean below,
aqua green . . .
Leaving one with the feeling
of serenity.
Eagles flying in the air
Otters swimming without a care.

Mountains surrounding,
all of this splendor . . .
Alaska, Alaska,
Your beauty mystified!

ALASKA'S MS RYNDAM
HOLLAND AMERICA LINE

"There is Magic
about being on a ship."
"A mobile city."

Sound of the Ocean,
near our door . . .
Such a feeling,
of Peace and Calmness.

Exciting,
formal dinners,
watching those wonderful Whales
from our window.

At night, all different,
shows on stage,
the last night, my favorite . . .
Broadway.

Top Deck-
"The Eagle's Crow's Nest,"
the most beautiful view,
God's glorious mountains and glaciers.

Indonesian People
with Grace, Charm, Kindness,
sang their farewell song,
our last night aboard.

Met an old woman, (on the ship)
Who said, "Enjoy Life,"
"Do all the things
you thought you were afraid to do."
"Do them before
your life is through."

****

About the Author

Dolores M. Miller is a poet and author living in Pennsylvania. Dolores lives with her Knight in Shining armor, Larry, and together they have two grown children, Larry (Jones) and Michele – who she loves with all her heart. The grandbabies Ella, Lilly and Victoria provide inspiration. All three are very much like their grandmother who loves to dance. In 2011, the newest addition was added to the family when baby Alex arrived on the scene.

Dolores is a compassionate, giving and loving person. In her writing she strives to convey the message of the human spirit to overcome adversity, see the beauty of nature and know God's healing love.

Dolores is also grateful for having had parents who adopted her out of a horrific situation. She is a survivor of childhood abuse. She says "there are so many children who are there most of their life." Making a difference through Child Advocates is rewarding and a source of beauty, love and healing for the community... and the world.

The Support Center for Child Advocates, aka Child Advocates has a special place in her heart. Each book sold benefits the Child Advocates. Net proceeds are donated to The Support Center for Child Advocates. The mission of Child Advocates is to advocate for victims of child abuse and neglect in Philadelphia with the goal of securing a permanent, nurturing environment for every child.

Child Advocates provides legal assistance and social service advocacy to abused and neglected children in Philadelphia. They seek to protect children by securing social services, finding alternative homes and helping them testify in court. For all the children committed to their care, they work to ensure safety, health, education, family permanency and access to justice.

For more information on

The Support Center for Child Advocates, please visit:
www.advokid.org

Publications and Awards

PUBLICATIONS & AWARDS
Partial listing

JMW Publishing Co. "The One" Poets of the New Millennium 2000

The National Library Of Poetry "From My Heart"(7th Love Letter) Best Poems Of The 90's

Book -"Another Dimension" Publisher: Sansip, Publishing Inc.1999

Tickled by Thunder "Winter Wonderland" Honorable Mention 1999

Short Story -"Anthony", Tickled by Thunder, 1999.

Sparrowgrass Poetry Forum, Inc, "Help One More Child Today", Poetic Voices Of America, Spring 1999

Witness To The Spirit "Did You See Her (Take The Time To Find Her)", 1999

Mutant Mule Review, "To You, Virginia Woolf", 1999

In Commemorating Excellence, By The National Authors Registry, Iliad Press, "Courage" 1998 President's Award

Tickled by Thunder "A NEW Epithet" and "Grace My Vancouver Friend" The Years Best Poems – 1998

The Bucks County Writer, "The Gazebo by the Sea" Published in the Summer, 1998

Poetry Guild, "I Left That Shore" A Celebration Of Poet's Showcase Edition, 1998

The National Library of Poetry, "Like The Dolphins" Outstanding Poets of 1998

Iliad Press "I Heard A Bird Chirping," The National Authors Registry 1998 –"The Browning Awards"

The National Library Of Poetry "God In Heaven"-Best Poems Of 1998

Awards
Award, Iliad Literary Award Program, "Courage" Winter 1997

Cader Publishing and Verses "A Touch Of Heaven," Honorable Mention – "Nature Award Program" 1997

International Poetry Hall of Fame, "Beauty" 1996

International Poetry Hall of Fame, "He Keeps Showing You The Way" 1996

International Poetry Hall of Fame, "Our Cousin Pat" 1996

In Commemorating Excellence, By The National Authors Registry, Iliad Press, "The Beautiful Warrior" President's Award 1995

PRAISE AND ACCOLADES

You are the Rarest of the Rare
You are a gem among women, a beautiful warrior, a pioneer, a woman of courage and strength, an essayist for modern times, a driving force in all our lives, a true friend, a diamond in the rough, the cream of the crop, the top of the heap... and, most importantly, a blessing in my life. All my love, on your birthday and everyday – Darlene

Enthusiasm
I wish that everyone had your enthusiasm for life! Thanks for all you do, but most of all for the spirit you bring to everything you do. - Sandra

Circle of Angels
Dolores, You are the reason hundreds of children each year are rescued from abuse and neglect. You are a lifeline of hope. From the bottom of our hearts we thank you for joining hands with us in our circle of compassion and protection for the children. - Sara O'Meara and Yvonne Fedderson

Touch My Soul
I so admire your strength to overcome pain. We don't know why bad things happen to us, but perhaps it is through pain we go outside of ourselves, and are able to reach out and help others. Maybe it makes us a better, more loving person. You are truly a beautiful warrior, and now you use your strength to defend those who need you. Perhaps without your pain, you would not have found God, and would not be the person you are. I hope you realize that others need your message of strength and hope. Your poem "Sweet Children Of War" is a favorite. Thank you for your words and for reaching out and sharing your feelings. In the short time we talked, you made a lasting impression on me. For me, you looked into my eyes and told me you saw strength and bravery there - and instantly I felt stronger and braver! Thank you – Jan

Special Gifts
You have so many special gifts and I am happy you are spending the time you deserve to work on your book. You have already helped so many, touched so many lives, and I know in the end your book will be fantastic, like you! Love Karen

Continuing Journey
I certainly have an awareness of the pain and suffering [you went through] in your life. I also am aware of how you transformed that pain into peace. – Michaeline

Dolores M. Miller
Poet & Author
Beautiful Warrior

www.beautifulwarrior.com

www.ingramcontent.com/pod-product-compliance
Lightning Source LLC
LaVergne TN
LVHW041634070426
835507LV00008B/617